ON WINGS OF WORDS

D1520015

Parvinder Mehta

Praise for *On Wings of Words*

"A refreshing new voice in South Asian diasporic poetry, Parvinder Mehta writes passionately about her Sikh faith, her identity as an academic, a mother, an immigrant, and a woman of color. These poems are united by their focus on social justice as they examine sectarian and racist violence against Sikhs in India and in the United States. The poems celebrate resilience and seek hope in community, memories, and faith."

-Professor Nalini Iyer, Professor of English, Seattle University, USA.

"With her debut volume of poems, On Wings of Words, scholar Parvinder Mehta joins the growing community of South Asian poets in North America. Many of Mehta's poems are responses to personal and political situations faced by members of the Sikh faith in India, the U.S., and elsewhere, but her poems are much more than just Sikh poems. They explore a wide variety of moods, stances, and experiences that are broadly human, even existential. If we were to read her poem, "Why We Write" as a putative manifesto, then the need to write, "to write to change," is an existential necessity. Mehta invites her readers to fly with her on wings of words, as they take in a sharp observation, a moment of gentle humor or satire, the memory of a loved one now gone, the joy of eating a mango in the rain, and so much more."

-Professor Amritjit Singh, Langston Hughes Professor Emeritus of English, Ohio University,USA.

"Reading Parvinder Mehta, an emerging poet of the Sikh diaspora and an accomplished scholar and teacher, I recalled the words of my mentor—*guru* in her cultural framework—William Carlos Williams: "It is difficult / to get the news from poems / yet [people] die miserably every day / for lack / of what is found there." Parvinder Mehta's poetry is necessary and affirmative in addressing the truth of poetry to what people die miserably every day of. She finds her examples ready to hand in the experiences of displacement and the historic persecution of the ethnic Sikhs in India and now in the United States. What convinces in her work is the steadfast unfolding of a nuanced voice, between American and subcontinental ways of speaking and rhythm, that builds power in comprehending and affirming—more than mere witnessing—the experiences she has emerged from, continues to name precisely, bringing the reader to awareness, fusing diasporic displacement with everyday life."

- Professor Barrett Watten, Wayne State University, USA

On Wings of Words
Copyright © 2021 Parvinder Mehta, Ph.D

ISBN 978-1-8381437-4-9

Printed in the United Kingdom by KhalisHouse Publishing
www.KhalisHouse.com
info@KhalisHouse.com

Find us on:
Instagram/KhalisHouse
Twitter/KhalisHouse

Khalis House
Publishing

For Manmohan, Monick & Mohull:
I write because you inspire me

In sweet memories of grandparents
who sought new homes
and dear parents who shared their
stories of displacements:

Amrit Kaur & Jaswant Singh Kohli
Kuldip Kaur & Amar Singh Mehta

Acknowledgements

This collection has been inspired from a lifelong love of poems that evoke emotions and challenge the mind to shatter its shackles. The list of poets whose work and ethos informs my work is too long to list here. I want to acknowledge the poetry of Sikh scriptures, Gurbani, that probably first drew me closer to the poetic form.

Written throughout more than a decade, some poems are evocative responses to this wonderous world, some highlight social injustice, while others are deeply personal reflections on the human condition. Some of the poems have appeared in literary anthologies, online magazines, and web blogs as well as personal social media sites and I want to thank so many who supported me in this journey. I want to acknowledge my thanks to T. Sher Singh and Harijot Singh Khalsa for providing me the initial platform for sharing some of my poems. More support came from mentors and fellow writers as Ishmeet Kaur Chaudhry, Roopali Sircar Gaur, Anita Nahal, Charanjeet Kaur, Amandeep Sandhu and Sandhya Suri in publishing and promoting my work. I am grateful for academic peers who acknowledged my writings by teaching them in their classes.

I am also thankful to the Humanities Center at Wayne State University for offering me the special Covid mini-grant which led to writing of the pandemic poems. Many thanks to Prof. Nalini Iyer, Prof. Amritjit Singh and Prof. Barrett Watten for their time in reviewing my manuscript and offering their endorsements.

I must thank my editor, Ranveer Singh, for his admirable patience throughout this whole process. Thanks to all my friends who shared their appreciation for my writings and encouraged me to keep writing more. In gratitude, I also want to acknowledge all my students who made me a better teacher and a learner throughout my teaching career. In many ways, you all have

i

validated my voice and belief in advocating our narratives and understanding from each other.

This book is the result of the deep love that I have received from my family and friends all over the world. My husband, Manmohan Mehta, and sons, Monick and Mohull Mehta, have been instrumental in enabling me to articulate my words with humility, empathy and kindness. Your persistent encouragement made this book happen. My relatives in India and elsewhere—sisters and brothers-in-law, nephews, nieces, cousins—have provided me the moral support and unconditional love which has nurtured and sustained me, living a diasporic life. Kanwal Preet Kochhar, Sarvjeet Kaur, Gursharan Kaur Anand, and Kulwant Bedi, your sisterly love and care makes me nostalgic for memorable times and hope for more loving moments of togetherness.

I hope these poems will touch some hearts and forge new relationships of readership.

Preface

As I imagine you perusing through these pages, I wonder what it is that you may want to know about me or about these words that have shaped me. These poems are a labor of love as well as pain, an indulgence that sometimes allowed me to respond quietly and at other times seek a voice or a clarion call so I could scream in the void of helplessness. I never imagined that I could write poems. Yet when I start writing poems, words whisper and nudge me to write them, flowing onto the blank screen as I imaginatively fly on their wings with different emotions so they can be validated. The power of words in evoking a mosaic of memories and feelings becomes almost a redemptive exercise for me. Poetry evokes in us our therapeutic needs to affirm our humanity and even offer an emotional redemption from the murkiness of an anxiety-ridden world. With an ongoing pandemic, dealing with crises of faith, feelings, and formations that continuously challenge us, poetry has now assumed a more pronounced function. Through words, we try to grasp the shimmeriness of the distant stars, reminding us of our distant memories of joy and loss from times bygone. Through words, we try to create an origami of comfort to help assuage the pain, loss, or grief surrounding us. Through words, we also find new silhouettes of hope in an overcast sublime. Through words, then I have tried to seek my lost homes, allowing myself to re-inhabit those ephemeral spaces of being, and hoping to affirm my various senses of being.

The poems in this collection were written over several years and have emotionally sustained me in many ways. I wrote the earlier poems feeling the need to affirm my identity which wavered between the need to question prejudice and intolerance and choose a transformative approach. The existential constraints that I felt growing up as a Sikh woman in India, structured within social expectations, seemed to extend over when I migrated with my husband to America. Living as a minority in India and then in America reminded me of how I was perceived through frames of otherness. I first began writing poems when I was an undergraduate student, newly exposed to the western literary tradition. Those poems were no poems, yet I cherish them – scribbles of emotion in blue ink on now faded pages of my notebook—for they made me believe that I have stories to tell, issues to highlight, and words to confirm myself and my community. I permitted myself to write blobs of text about a particular emotion and then tried to scratch out those extra trimmings, those haphazard ruminations that went directionless, finally canceling the whole chunk with an x-mark. These words remained visible even in their scribbled, scratched foreground. Even in their canceled state, they remind me of that time when I started believing in my nascent creativity.

My poetry is also a homage to my parents whose influence on me has been indelible in becoming a lifelong learner. I consider these poems like the intricate patterns of a crocheted lacework. The gentle purls and knits and the patient transferring of thread onto the pointed needles as they slowly extend the design remind me of the creativity that I learned from my mother when I was a young teenager. She taught me the art of knitting, not poetry. Throughout her academic career as a teacher and a high school principal, she encouraged me to imagine a career in academia. During summer breaks when I had more time, she would teach me how to knit and crochet. Yet even though I stopped knitting as I got mired in the world of academia, poetry offered me a reason to continue knitting with words instead of needles. To imagine a beauty, grace, and modesty that my mother exemplified, I found solace after her passing in the words that I imagined she would whisper in my ears, "yes, now remove these words gently from the needle of this sentence and purl them on the other needle. Wait and see; the design will come up for sure!" And so, in grieving loss, I found the silent courage to begin writing poems, but they were not meant to be read yet. Whenever I write a poem, I ask myself, "Would my mother like it if she was still with me?" And so, I try to knit and purl words with emotions hoping to please my mother, imagining her sweet smile widening her lips with acknowledgment and pride. "Yes, you got it right!

It's beautiful!" From my father, I learned to adapt to new surroundings yet seek our narratives instead of borrowed ones and build a community of thinkers who provoke and persuade you to shift your paradigms. As a professor, he loved saying, "We should discuss the arguments and learn from them." In writing these poems, I also seek to discuss some arguments and imagine how my father would have responded to them: with pride but also with numerous questions about diasporic lives, and displaced identities.

In many of these poems, I have imagined missed conversations and have looked for a home that is gone now yet is still there somewhere. The imaginary homes that draw us to the mires of history, memory, nation, and more are traceable in these poems about displacement and arrival, erasures and acknowledgments, and silences and voices. These poems concentrate on the relationship between words and feelings to reflect my experiences of living in a world with an otherness forged through multiple homes, migrations and identities. Sometimes the predicament of growing up as a Sikh girl in non-Sikh spaces reminds me of the displacement that my ancestors experienced in myriad ways. My parents were young children when the 1947 partition happened and they were forced to leave their homes in undivided Punjab, seek refuge, and build newer homes in independent India. How did they, as children, cope with their memories and losses of earlier homes? I re-imagine their resilience to grow roots in new homes, affirm their senses of being, and emulate their optimism. So, on wings of words, I aim to soar high and give a voice to the quiet murmurs and unheard sighs seeking an audience.

Parvinder Mehta
Detroit, Michigan
21st October 2021

Feelings

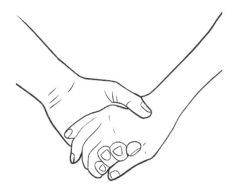

No evidence!

Yes, there is ample evidence of racism...
If only you could see, hear, and feel.

You don't see with your myopic,
impaired eyes those systems of
oppressions that enabled you
to climb up while disabling others.

You don't hear those
punches of entitlement
in playgrounds and sidewalks
bruising minds and more
with mottles of blued bloody scars
on brown, yellow and black bodies.

You don't feel the trauma
that jumps upon those innocents
getting violated and attacked for
their differences, queer and otherwise.

So, before you claim no evidence of racism
look at the mirror and its hidden
cracks from which you justify your
hate that you inherited yet deny
with your golden privilege and silver spoons.

Waves

A mass shooting brings swelling waves
of shock gnashing against boulders of hate,
of performative statements about victimhood
of history lessons about our value and struggle
of debates about guns and white supremacy
of thoughts and prayers for our grieving hearts
of candlelight vigils to prove our humanity,
even of neoliberalism and its solidarity
through hashtags, crowdfunding and t-shirts,
of slacktivists monetizing their opportunism
with templates of borrowed wisdom and
simulated metaphors of dreams and freedom.

And then the waves recede quietly,
passively leaving grim residues
of heavy unspoken grief for the injustice
of whispering sighs of guilt and mourning
of lingering traumas of surviving hate
of painful losses caused by the hateful shooter.
And like washed up empty seashells drenched
in drowning despair, we pray for new mornings
seeking courage to heal our gaping wounds
with fearless compassion and dry our tears
to imagine a better world where no abhorrent
shooter ever thinks of a mass shooting again.

A Prayer

May we be empowered to embrace kindness for all
May we be drenched with colors of compassion for all
May we rejuvenate our commitment to all
Regardless of who we are, what we wear,
How we speak, how we love, and how we live.
In humility and grace, to cherish this life,
May we leave a beautiful legacy of inclusion for all.

This is the hope that we bring on...
A better, kinder world for all
To soothe us so we feel and see
life's beauties instead of getting mired
in whose world is the best of all.

On Reading Poetry

Oh, the wonders of reading poetry!
Such a calligraphy of emotions the cornea
comes upon, eyes kissing the black alphabets,
caressing each word as a passing train.
The mind marvels at the stealthy meaning
embracing its labyrinths. The lips quiver at
the gushing emotions like a blushing bride.
Fingers nervously itching to turn the page
wondering about consummation. A smile,
a twitch, a frown, a brow rises in surprise,
doubt, even amazement. Words breathe and
conduct an invisible choreography
of feelings satiated. The reader finally
composed by this composition, an emboldened
lover bursting with ecstasy.

Words hanging on a clothesline

Words hanging on a clothesline,
half-uttered, half-dried
swaying in the air
between thought and utterance
beck me, peck me
see them, translate those
wet splotches before they
evaporate into vacuous nothingness.

How her red tunic bleeds over
the embroidered petulance
despite reassurances of commitment,
swaying in air yet firmly held in its place
by that stubborn clothespin merely half an
inch from his black corduroy pants.
The red fails to bleed over darkness of black,
it simply embarrasses smearing
its own self, quietly creating an unwanted
smudge. Her pink eye-laced *duppatta*
tries to flirt with his checkered shirt
caressing over its back spread out.
Yet it slings off and cuddles itself
on a lonely, cramped corner
wrinkled by insistent rejections.

Words damp with sorrow
cling heavily to the line
as other emotions fly lightly over
burdensome thoughts
over layering sorrow with
transparent consoling and chimeric caresses
as the wind blows kisses and sucks
the words to dry up into a soft-spoken
surrender of silent serendipity.

Broken mirrors

Before you eagerly scream and protest,
in tone-deafness, listen to our
resonant silences and hoary whispers
– frustrations of our mind-forged manacles.

Before you walk out in demand
without compassion and redress,
stand still and note our unprivileged conditions
–alienations of our mind-forged manacles.

Before you resist visible implications
of our differences, heed to our invisibilities
and desperate urgencies that seek address
– vulnerabilities of our mind-forged manacles

finally leaving shards of broken mirrors everywhere.

Thinking about thinking

The more I think,
the more the thought untangles me.
I wander in the labyrinthian maze,
And every dead-end comes alive
with possibilities!
What a cat and mouse game–
the tussles and tangles of thoughts
bring smiles with contentment at
this loving surrender.
I learn my ignorance
and ignore my knowledge.

On finishing grading

O the joys of finishing my grading!
No more worries of plagiarists presuming
innocence while denying their criminality.
No more wonder at the callous stupidity
of borrowed words simply brimming
with arrogance. Yet, so often, I am amazed by
those prodigious insights that diligent
minds display in their thoughtful labyrinths.
My eyes lit up with brilliance as my reading
brings me to a flourishing end of contented
learning like watching a beautiful peacock
dancing after the rain.

Raw Impulses

The roads do not question the travelers,
selflessly taking us to our destination.
winding and coiling in anticipation,
the ultimate end.

The flowers do not ask us about our Gods
merely pleasing with fragrance and beauty,
blooming and withering in silent acknowledgement,
of that eternal beauty.

The air we breathe does not ask us our faith,
simply looming and then abating.
filling up empty worlds,
willing to subsume all that matters.

The rain that drenches us does
not pick and choose, showering
all willful souls, immersing and
seeping our bodies with peace.

A child's cry, piercing the heart,
looking for that comfort and re-assurance
for a world not lost,
does not inquire the listener's devotion.

Why does it then matter
when a man venerates differently,
when a woman believes another divinity?

O why have we forgotten these raw impulses,
these inner essences?
Why can't our humanity, our worship transcend the
prejudices of symbols?
If only we could, if only we could...

Why We Write

We write ...
because words peck us, beck us
to reveal those unsaid secrets.
Because grief trickles and prickles
like a cold ice-cube melting
to purge the sadness and tears within.
Because milk that is spilt crosses all limits
meandering to escape its spatial prison
to leave blotches after hurried erasures.
Because thoughts and prayers fail
and fizzle to evoke the necessary kindness
unless we write and change,
unless we change and write.

We write...
because words inspire a passionate
lovemaking in joy to elevate the minds
reading those words kissing imagination
and that imagination kissing beauty.
Because ecstasy evokes and provokes
a blushing bride embracing those loving arms
wanting to declare her love on the rooftops.
Because happiness shimmers
and glimmers those sparkles of emotion
like fireflies in a summery night
appearing in a flash and disappearing
in a resounding heartbeat.

We write...
because life traps us in its labyrinths
with those clutches of confusion
and like a blind, anxious mouse

sniffing its way through the maze
we walk carefully on eggshells
where the burning ambers are hissing softly
that burnt smell of dreams undreamt.
Because hope nudges and grudges catching sunny rays
that fight with the angry clouds to somehow
find its way out of the tiring, dark hodgepodge.
Because we must birth out painful echoes
whispering in dark agony to come out and be heard.

We write...
Because our words are not there
hidden like invisible histories and unexplored pasts
undocumented as sediments of non-being
or evaporating leaving mere smudges of despair.
We collect alphabets, and words and sew them,
knit them, purl them with threads and yarns
of emotions, with hope and faith
which then glitter and adorn
our bare necks with our dissenting necklaces
marked with beauty and scars of our ancestors
who dreamed about this and so much more—
to leave that legacy of starry stamps on skies.

We write and we write
Until words soothe us with comfort and wave to us
Until thoughts slip into meanings and nod approvingly to
us.
Until love gives itself to us and inspires life in us.
Until you read our words and finally understand us.

Blue aerograms

Papa, I wish I had seen you one last time
before the flames of grief took you away.
One last glimpse of your eyes closed forever
of your smiles that departed when your body
gave up on the ventilator and medical revival.
You left me way before the world became small
before the Facetimes and What'sApps
before even emails that dinged with instant love.
I read those blue aerograms that you sent
me every month till you could not
anymore because aneurysms are
quicker than aerograms. So you live on
in my readings of your letters.
My treasure of wishes and blessings,
the paper has become fragile,
its glue a distant memory,
yet your words in Chelpark ink
soothe me always and will do so till
my last breath when I hope to see you again.

On reading a scholarly book

When the mind reads those intellectual ramblings
defining complicated nuances of a field,
the maze of struggles and challenges of canon
the entangling politics of representation
and dubious traps of misrepresentations,
I marvel at the hard labor
scholars bring to affirm the significance
of their work, those long, silent engagements
those carefully nourished intellectual pregnancies
finally birthing a love – a book bound by ideas
and unbound by possibilities.

A New Threshold

Another threshold crossed today,
another moment to cherish today.
From the moment of your first walk
when you entered these hallways
learning to trust your teachers,
you stand today as proud, fearless players.
You have now learned those moves
of poise, and calm dexterity, walking today
with a regal confidence.

May you fly high like a kite in the air
relishing the cool caresses of knowledge,
enjoying the melodies of life.
May the wings of your beautiful minds,
flutter like a butterfly out from this
cozy cocoon and soar you up
high in bright colors.
May the dreams of your life
embrace you with kindness and warmth.

As you tread gently upon life's meadows
look not just at the luscious grass,
but also, those tiny, colorless dews that just be.
Do not simply gaze the distant bright stars
also admire those half-luminous crescents
glimmering nearby. Cherish these
precious moments of learning.
Keep soaring like a kite,
keep dancing to the music of life.
Rule the hearts with passion,
rule the hearts with smiles.

When Poems Are Born

A blank page invites
to scribble my thoughts,
figuring out jaunty emotions
as alphabets dash out happily
in a chorus of creativity
displaying a choreography between
thoughts and emotions, words and phrases
evoking melodies of sensual and sacred.
The mind ruminates on raw rhapsody
in tinkling of anklets when the dancer taps her feet
or of a nervous, shy bride claiming happiness
and creates a rainbow of feelings– fleeting and flickering
memories sewn with imagination of things to come.
A poem emerges as words and more words
snuggle together in sheer ecstasy of
being born with new meanings.

A blank page reminds me
to carve those labyrinths of passive witnessing
as alphabets crawl out in painful shock
displaying the swallowing fissure between
aphasia and acknowledgement
evoking a numb necessity to narrate.
The mind ruminates on raw cruelty
like birthing pains of a mother forced to be
her body stretched within and pain without.
Or like violated men tortured,
drowning in their own pools of blood
ravaged by pain strewn together
as a patchwork of sighs and whispers.
Another poem forces out as words and more words
comfort each other in sheer anguish of
silence about trauma of bygone darkness.

Eating mangoes on a rainy day

Oh, what a pleasure it was –
eating mangoes in the rain
under a canopy in the verandah.
Mangoes—yellow, ripe and luscious
Rain—voluptuously drenching, kissing
the hard, granite floor.

Oh, what a symphony of senses—
that mingling of sounds, sweet smells,
scrumptious symphonies, an unheard
saga of love, contours of soft succulence
surrendering to sheer, innocent pleasure.

Oh, what a torrential joy–
Raindrops smashing
the concrete and trying to fly back up,
droplets hurriedly trying to caress
while you seduce the deep yellow
ripeness melting in your mouth.

Oh, what simple lessons—
cool mesmerizing splashes
reminding of life's vitality,
to behold a supreme sense of
surrender. To be alive, to feel beauty
of the body and the everlasting soul.

Remembering My Friend[1]

I lost her to unexplained reasons,
fumbling, rummaging, delving,
grappling with queries, I wonder why.
Shock batters my mind,
words of reasons choke me
in silence. The whys and what ifs
struggling out of unspoken stillness,
fearsome speculations, unasked questions,
untold answers, nudge me to think
about him. Could he? Did he? But why?
How could he? His tranquil demeanor and kind charm
seemed a perfect match to her serene smiles.
Their grace still etched in memories
of gatherings, celebrations, prayers, chance
meetings, entailed in this diasporic friendship.

My mind wanders to those earlier days before
motherhood, when we learned kirtan together.
Tracing melodies on the harmonium, our voices,
learning rhythms of blissful lyrics, nervous fingers
careful with caution not to slip on the wrong note.
Singing those blessed lyrics of love, compassion,
separation, and divine reunion, we became sisters
in music, simply following notes of life with
care, hopes and aspirations.

I still remember—
those glimmering eyes when
she welcomed her first-born, sharing

---

[1] This poem recalls a friend, who along with her two young sons, was
allegedly killed by her husband in an apparent case of murder-suicide.

birthing joys and growing pains with
graceful gratitude. That smile when she
congratulated me for new motherhood,
still warms my heart. That affection at their
housewarming, the symphony of thanksgiving
as we celebrated their new home, and joys
of parenthood linger in pleasant recall.
Those walls with beautiful family pictures,
canvasses of memories, sculptures of art
and souvenirs from happy travels, materialize
those images from past. That charming
voice of her first-born proudly reciting speeches
to large audiences, impressing them with marvel
and pride, still echoes in annals of the mind.
Those goodbyes when she moved on to a
new city in hopes, wishes, ambitions for
better prospects— I remember it all,
I remember it all.

I refuse to imagine –
those tears and screams
when death assaulted them
those last moments of horrible cognition,
the guilt of departure, shame and extinction.
I see her, not as a victim, a statistic.
I see her not in the borrowed picture with
 frozen smiles. I see her not in the horror
of painful battery and cruel termination.
 I see her instead in nostalgic memories of
heartwarming moments – of kindness, service
and thankful acknowledgements.

I see her in the perennial daisies
with pristine charm, surrendering to ephemeral

life. No blame, no guilt, no question marks.
Bidding farewell, left with strands of her memories,
I smell those daisies, cherishing fragrant moments
when her smiles brightened us all. Resting in peace
in that eternal abode, I imagine her singing those
lyrics of the soul. Divine love embracing her,
no care, no worry, all in spiritual bliss and heavenly
grace. Only love subsuming everyone
Goodbye my friend, goodbye...
farewell my friend, rest in peace.

Violence

The Plight of a Shadow

They come every year
asking me the same questions:
"How did it happen?
How did you deal?
Can we have a picture?
A sad face will look real!"
I have become a stone
to their pelting queries.
Hard grief penetrates
again and again. A broken
sculpture re-sculpted
to fit their mold. An image,
of burning now blurred beyond
memory, hammered by grief,
chiseled with loss haunts me,
yet they ask me again to describe
my feelings and anger.

Between the image and the words
the horror and the emotions
there is a bulwark of reality
asking me other questions.
How will I get my children their
next meal? Will my son's miseries
end his life sooner? What is the future
of my daughter's traumatic past?
They never ask these questions.
Stuck in that forced, desiccated past
plastered upon me, they try to peel off
dry layers in hopes of finding something
new. The dead stone keeps growing
nourished with this barrage of queries,

a dead cocoon and a dead gaze
only shows a barren ground
trampled upon by curious explorers
hoping to discover ignored histories
and painful memories.

They fruitlessly ask me about them-
the killers that ageing justice can't see
anymore. These naïve reporters know not
their predecessors who also
asked, wrote yet failed like them.
Those dusty police files, pages torn
lest hideous secrets be revealed,
are submerged in cobwebs of apathy
and hollow compassion.
Justice knows not me
nor my plight. She simply left me,
a mere shadow of a dark past,
a mystery that will never see the light.

A Dream Still Deferred[2]

I saw the grieving young kid on TV
expressing sorrow he didn't know before
nostalgic for that last maternal meal
chewed, swallowed with tears
that last bite of her tangible love.
Blue somberness, black grief
recalling a future denied
by festering hate that snatched
her arms for support,
her hands for comfort foods
her smiles for celebrations
her shoulder for solace.
Nervous, controlled emotions
carefully measured words
touching listeners who
choked and gulped their tears,
gasping for pure air
amidst polluting abhorrence.
Questioning the dream that he wanted
that she wanted, he asks for forceful words,
and compassion to combat hate.
Will we stand with him so he can
hope, seek and demand
a dream still deferred?

---

[2] This poem is inspired from Harpreet Singh Saini's address on hate crimes to the US Senate Judiciary Subcommittee. Harpreet's mother, Paramjit Kaur Saini, was one of the 6 people fatally shot to death in a mass shooting by a white supremacist at the Sikh Gurdwara in Oak Creek, Wisconsin in August 2012.

"Racism does not exist…"

But, oh yes, it does—
In the eyes of those stares,
In the words of those dares,
In the logic of those reasons
that blame the victims
without questioning the
power-wielding supremacy.

And, oh yes, it does—
In those imperatives to change
unfamiliar names, and languages,
unfamiliar layers of being,
unfamiliar lossbecause the majority must rule
to define what is and not for ridicule.

And, still, it does—
despite those accommodations
those whitening assimilations
those morphic tolerances
to abide and follow white-washed
inferences to cower under power
and implicitly know all along
that yes, racism does exist!

Difficult Times

It must be difficult times
farmers becoming warriors
-their cudgels of activism
burrowing into numb, fallow minds
seeking an equitable world
that nourishes all not some,
fighting a quiet battle for justice
for those in man-made panopticons
feeling the pain of a distant freedom
denied, a broken promise of words.

It must be difficult times
teachers becoming soldiers
-saving young lives from sudden dangers
those desks of learning, closets and classrooms
becoming bunkers and shelters from hate
crouching students hiding in fear
notebooks smeared in blood
broken spectacles helplessly abandoned
feeling the terror of vengeful
aggression on scapegoat victims.

It must be difficult times
citizens protesting violent authorities
-holding placards and hands up in the air
remembering victims of misdirected safety
rallying that which should be
rebelling that which should not be
feeling the suffocation of racial prejudice
dissenting chokeholds of control
hoping to breathe a freedom
that they must have always.

It must be difficult times
when children of a different God,
a different race, a different nation
cannot nurture hope, seek peace,
cannot inhale kindness or seek solace
cannot feel pure unadulterated love
because fumes of toxic hate simply
refuse to acknowledge their smiles
their wonders, their curiosities to
learn of a better world
even in their raw sense of humanity.

It must be difficult times
others becoming more others
having to prove their solidarities
sustaining their self-identities
affirming customary differences
clarifying themselves for those powerbrokers
who simply don't feel the need to love
who simply don't wish to desire,
to wave and welcome them
to know them and their humanity.

If only it weren't so, if only it weren't so!
If only the farmers were free
If only the teachers were free
If only the citizens were free
If only the children were free
If only the others were free
To dream a better world,
inhaling a sweet kindness
That imbues us all in gratitude for
a beautiful world of beautiful minds.

Disappeared

No present, no future
only a version of narrated past
stoked with danger, terror
and labels of otherness
before they too disappear.

No family, no friends
only grieving mute survivors
hissing quiet tears of grief,
mourning their trauma
before they too disappear.

No news, no reporting
only accusations of fanaticism
and rebellion for speaking out,
creating hoary whispers
before they too disappear.

No apology, no acknowledgement
only invisible hope for memories
of those snatched souls
living quietly with unmet justice
before they too disappear.

Oak Creek: Mementos, Memorials, Marathons

Years have passed by since
their voices were hushed.
We remember them amidst
mementos of remembrance
manifestos of recognition
mirrors of reflection
memorials of reminiscences
even marathons of reconciliation.
No wallowing wailing to subsume
rueful actions nor eulogies to yearn
those unheard voices, only strong wishes
will affirm our humanity. A chorus of
melodious optimism percolates
immaculate insights in seekers
of a better loving world
devoid of rancid revulsion
 insular xenophobia
and vacuous fears.
No words of vandalism
smeared in blind hatred
can drown this soaring spirit.
Moving on with resilience,
beyond comatose inabilities,
the resonant refrain of
compassion, service, and oneness
will echo and be heard.
Hoping those eyes blinking in
passive silence today will soon gleam and
pronounce "chardi kala" and bring
peace for all.

Beyond Unspoken Words[3]

Their taunts and foul looks,
hurtful shards of haunting slurs
seek to depress me to non-being.
The barrage of forceful punches,
the onslaught of knuckles and
those deliberate toggles to defeat me,
aim for my surrender to non-essence.
They attack me and my looks, an unfamiliar Sikh,
a paraphernalia beyond speculation.

Do I dare explain myself to them?
 speak to those resounding, deaf ears
make them see their ill-illumined dungeons?
Why don't they learn to know me?
Why don't they know to learn me?
I roll my life – a crumpled paper
hidden in a deep pocket, crushed and
marked beyond recognition.

Holding onto this useless fragment
 I lay it open in privacy.
Caressing its innocent creases
I recall those dangerous moments,
those arrows of hateful glances
and spears of vicious words,
those smirks while chewing meaningless gum,
those gibes at my long cherished hair,

---

[3] This poem is a response to numerous real-life incidents of bullying
against young minds aspiring to learn in life. The narrator is imagined
as a young, Sikh teenager boy who comes to terms with his
experiences of bullying through affirmation, history, and art.

and my curly black beard. They left invisible
fault lines on this paper, ingrained
with smudges beyond erasure.

Their onslaught on my being
rattled my body yet crushed not its spirit.
Their pouncing on my head to tousle
my patka, exposed my hair to their cruel
gaze of mockery and apathy.
My soft silky hair undone, shield my eyes from
their repugnance and repulsive wonderment.
They leave me alone with a puzzled look,
the cracked mirror in the locker shows me,
my reflections disfigured beyond repair.

Somehow, my faith confirms a steadfast
refusal to assimilate to their demands
of conformity. I walk the hallways
hoping for acceptance and freedom,
like naked feet avoiding the pierce of a
sharp broken glass. Those glances of
scrutiny fail to shake me as my iron bracelet
reminds me of resolve and affirming allegiance.
The teachers look at me as a puzzle
a riddle they never can know,
a strange artifact for their gaze, simply a
darkness of a cavernous maze
an intricacy beyond learning.

At home, I hold onto my life – these wasted papers
my globes of insignificant secrets,
collecting every day, unfolding their
crushed fragilities, caressing the wounds of
markedness and then binding them all together.

These shapeless spheres have mingled with
each other's pain and hurt. The caressing
fingers at last found a meaning in this
origami of comfort beyond pain.

New shapes of resolve and firmness
appear magically as I begin to write
those hushed words and silent whispers.
Words spilling out of the rims of my heart,
their calm fury reminds me those other histories
of persecutions, of unknown strangeness
refusing to give in to tortures,
pressures of conversion and assimilation,
finding a way to define themselves
through sacrifice, rebellion and martyrdom,
a combat beyond oppression.

Remembering those subjections,
conversions, beheadings and declared deaths,
those histories of martyrdom and warriors,
I caress my wounds hidden in these globs of rejection,
patting their tattered folds every day.
Whispering the faint quivering of my heart,
I renew it with inner optimism.
A single tear seeps through
percolating the pain of histories
releasing bottled rage through blotted
letters as blue ink submerged in red
anger flows over, undrawing those marks of
miscognition, creating another art,
a calligraphy beyond rejection.

I wonder and hope for the day,
when they would value my existence,

know my reasons, my affirmations without
boxing me into orthodoxy or insularity.
My history of subjugation, meanwhile
nourishes my wounded soul,
as words emerge amidst blots of
grief and heal my unspoken pain.
Perhaps I am strong and tested,
perhaps I will win this battle
or perhaps I will be a martyr
beheaded by hate and oppression.
Till then I must go on
And follow my inner guidance
cherishing my heritage,
refusing to give in to injunctions and oversights
refusing to submit to recurrent oppression,
I will rise instead nobly as a young eagle
bravely learning to fly.
I will sing the clarion call to others
to shed the cacophony of jarring
hateful words and instead embrace
the mellow rhythms and musical strokes
creating a new art and articulation
beyond unspoken words.

A Dream of Pleas

I saw them in a dream
pleading against decapitation,
against packaging into fancy pieces,
laying in transparent coffins,
labeled freshly cut, boneless,
best used within six months.
The gluttonous reaper stuffed
it into an edible, helpless thing.

I saw them in a dream
pleading against skinning,
getting raped with buckles,
nails and heels. Wrapping around
in an embrace of skinny death.
An expensive accessory after
its own murder. The popular
diva flashed her soft skinned
shoulder with shimmering
cruelty dangling in mortal grip.

Then came another dream
where they came on to me,
haunting me, torturing me,
badgering me with words,
and their insomniac nightmares.
I know those eyes of pleas
finally lashing their anger at me.

I plead for my life.
I plead them to listen
and allow me to interject
But they decide to kill me,

cut me, skin me, and stuff me
With their collective gaze
of cumulative anger that
multiplied and never stopped.

Growling and howling,
hungry, greedy, reckless,
they clawed me, pawed me,
sawed me and jawed me.
I could not escape from this
brutality of consumption,
so horrified that I finally woke up.

"Bad ideas"

To unlearn our prejudices
To review our myopia
To question blind hate
To recognize our blind spots
To quieten our cacophony
To listen to otherness
To rethink prior lessons
and germinate kindness for all
are not bad ideas.

How Many More Candlelight Vigils?

I see those youthful smiles
and feel the tears for
those bonds, those friendships,
those promises, those hopes for
a better world, cut short by
cold, vicious agendas, blind
to our own mortality.

What words matter, what counsel
to abhorrent minds that only see
the surface and not the core
of our humanity?
To imagine those mournful screams
loudly choking with helpless loss,
pelting the grieving hearts
I hope silently for some harmony.

Do I dare apologize for our silent
reticence of these troubled times?
Do I fear the hate-mongers
seeking oblivious victims?
How many more candlelight vigils,
How many more solidarities
do we need to affirm?

With tears in my eyes, I know I must
find a kinder meaning, clinging on this
hope to confirm the sanctity of
those relations and bonds,
those friendships, those promises,
those hopes for a better world.

Colors of Fury

I

I remember that November morning
of contagious logic, when earth-shaking
reasoning spread like wildfire.
Genocidal ambition counted heads,
killed Sikhs in blind revenge and
mayhem with kerosene,
bamboos, and daggers.
Hiding, peering through cracks of dark curtain
I watched the horror and spectacle—
a man immersed in flames.
His hand withering painfully,
reaching out to remove the burning tire
that clutched his neck, melting his dreams.

The burning man's mother,
froze in shock as chilly flames of fury swallowed
her son into nothingness. Alone in
this circle of cruelty, she tried to douse
those hateful flames and reclaim her
loving son. The blazing demons
of prejudice consumed him
amidst heart-wrenching
shrieks and wails.

They kicked the mother away,
a loud thud and a cracked skull
finished her like a bug.
Vacant eyes dilated beyond
comprehension. Her fiery arms
lay motionless and barren.

Unmoored from this
world of rancid misconceptions
she watched me and my deathly fear.
I began to tremble,
What would happen to me?
Will they burn me, cut my hair
and worse, violate me?
The burning man, no stranger,
but their Sikh neighbor, a brother they
embraced on Diwali and hugged on Holi.
He now played alone with
the sputter of flames and colors of fury.

My eyes transfix and sway,
seeing this inhuman disgrace.
The burning man shrinking and sizzling
in an unconscious hush.
Lulled to sleep by the black smoke
finally embracing him. The smolders
continued to peck and tease as if appeasing a
cranky child into subservience.
The silent smoke hushed him
with blazing kisses, its maternal
lullaby calming him to silence
and eternal sleep. Preparing him to meet
his ultimate maker as a tearful mother
sends her bridal daughter away.

Delhi streets, strangely empty
strangely flooded. People watching
from the rooftops this spectacle of
disconnect and disaster, their safe
premises, and non-Sikh identities
no danger to their witnessing.

Mother smoke comforted many burning Sikhs
into eternal sleep. They checked the list,
preparing for the next burn, the next rape
moving into the inner alleys of inhumanity.
My edgy fingers transfixed, refused to release
the curtain to this drama of spectacle,
the unimagined wonder of human cruelty.

II

Thirty-seven years later, driving through these
highways, when smoke comes out
of unnamed buildings, it reminds me of him,
forever burning, engulfed by the smoldering
fury long forgotten. It reminds me of her,
forever trying to save her son
yet failing desperately. I wonder if she was asking
me for retribution or empathy. That shroud of passive
witnessing chokes me up with tears and whispers
of unheard silence. Perhaps another Sikh is
targeted with another vicious reasoning
of attacking minds and bodies,
of annihilating faith and beliefs.
These abandoned buildings with boarded
windows remind me of those abandoned
memories and boarded grief, of un-cremated
anguish and unuttered penitence.

Do I dare remember or forever burn
in this purgatory of hatred, and prejudice?
Are they still lurking in secret?
checking their lists, looking for more
victims? Crushing the rebellion of identity
cornering affirmation to fringes of abandon,

will they always repress, pursue and eradicate
newer philosophies, different ideologies?

III

Another country, another century
the horrendous twin destruction,
people burning in, imploding,
exploding hatred and depths of horrors.
Shrouds of concrete and toxic balms
smearing thousands with anguish.
Suits covered in black soot
running in a vacuous landscape,
looking for familiar places and streets
in that maze of unknown danger.
Ash-filled faces marked
with the horror of coming out alive,
the living ghosts of a labyrinthine limn.

Deathly smoke embraced many,
pacified some shrieking souls
while others jumped to lifelessness
to escape those unmotherly flames
and the burden of utter collapse.
Some rescued, others crushed in
frantic frenzy. Contagious destruction
seeped through, mediating horror
upon otherness through electronic images
and repetitive paranoia.

The persecution began again,
of unknown minds and head-coverings,
turbans and hijabs. Men in blue turban-spotting,
pushing and dragging a Sikh man

traveling alone on a subway.
Suspicion flickering from all directions
enveloping minds with surreal doubt.
Fumes of anger sizzling, haunted the
darker otherness to conceal their differences
and reveal only the red, white and blue.
The guilt of difference, those glares
demanded fidelity and patriotism
we had already assumed
as stepchildren in this new homeland.

He came out of nowhere to punish the
turban wearing step-citizens. Driving to the
gas-station, he shot the Arizona Sikh man planting
flowers to beautify like other Americans.
He snatched the Sikh's life, uprooting
him from the American landscape of
familiar whiteness. No need for turbans.
"Long live our nation!" he simply said,
moving on to eradicate another turbaned
otherness and then disappearing in darkness.

Sikh children marked strangers
in corridors of learning. Pushing, snatching
Sikhs' turban off, they twisted
black hair out of concealment,
wounding pride, injuring honor
and esteem of these warriors
of today's racial warfare. Forced,
some lost their pride to fear,
others lost their lives to fearlessness,
choosing simply to sacrifice against oppression.

Another afternoon slithered another killer

with agenda. Snooping with rage
he watched those two old Sikhs,
walking on the sidewalk
enjoying the cool California air.
Their bliss of retirement,
their children's affection
brought them to this no Sikh-man's land.
Reminiscing about their childhoods,
their adopted homeland
how it had changed them,
and framed them on the sidewalks of
an indifferent suburbia.
Walking in reminiscence, pondering
memories of their homeland
that was not and the homeland that
couldn't be. Their flowing grey beards,
aging bodies made them easy
targets and victims. He shot them to death,
retiring them prematurely from this life
and its inconsistent tragedies.

Again, he came with his vicious,
suicidal agenda and toxic mindset
killing those Wisconsin worshippers
in service. Barging in sanctimonious
blindness into the welcoming sanctuary,
in fleeting moments destroying six lives
of hopes, dreams, and despair. A single
moment dissolved his ethical responsibility,
ending his life uncaringly. The tears of injustice
choking everywhere.

Disappearing as a shadow
in light, he might still

emerge again and again and then
again. Another reason or cause,
another misdirected wrath
a hollow, dark tunnel, might bring him
back like a nightmare waiting to
pounce upon our slumberous humanity.
His misguided frenzy for foreigners
too dark for candlelight vigils
and memorials. Sikh targets
on a street, in a car, in a plane implicated
in the "us and them" rhetoric. A passive
perpetuation of robotic, repetitive paranoia
of their strangeness. A shadow in the light,
a shadow in the light.

This strange feeling, a dismal sense
of cornucopia brings questions
of motives, reasons, conflicts
of unresolved intentions.
Shocking grief and aphasia of
incoherence bothers like an open
wound pinching, seeking care.

IV

They do not understand
those traditions and histories,
those memories and chronicles
of sacrifices and affirmation,
brave resistance and resilience,
to conversion and assimilation.
Forgetting their own persecutions,
their conquered aggressions,
their controlling conversions,

their fickle memories erase their
own houndings. The festered sores of
prejudice explode the aneurysm
of ethnic hate erupting volcanic ash
and xenophobic embers.

I imagine the mother of the Sikh man
alive today. Smiling with optimism, caressing
his long, black hair that never singed in
those flames of fury. Her delicate fingers
kneading coconut oil into the tender,
black roots as his hair glimmer with hope.
Untangling those wavy strands from tethers of
an ignored mesh, she eyes me, assures me
and says "chardi kala." The gas-station
owner too smiles as his hands caress a
delicate plant placing it firmly in the new landscape.
Assured of roots merging with the rich soil,
his tulips, marigolds and the beautiful
cacti, all shimmer with an amazing grace.
I also see those Sikh men walking
on the sidewalk again. Their rhythmic
steps, without fear or concern,
tread with optimism. Cool air brushing
their grey beards. They are at home finally
growing roots in a new home. The Wisconsin
worshippers also smile in contentment
of service, blissful in the divine sanctuary.
They assure me to be fearless
to come out and release this
curtain of passive witnessing
and remembrance. I must reveal the
shroud of ignorance. Speak their
unheard voices. Together we must

learn to tolerate turbans, flowing beards.
Together we must embrace ethnic garbs
and marks. Together we must educate errors,
open history's sealed windows to edify,
finally dissipate those burning flames
and dissolve these colors of fury.

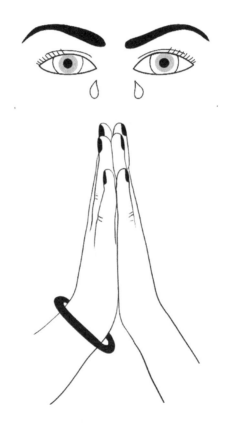

Waris

Their eyes filled with suspicion
screening for potential danger
fail to see his humanity. Their gaze
of mistrust denies him approval, and
insists on random searches
again, and again. He hopes they will
learn about him, understand him.
Someday they will...

Some kind eyes may politely
plead for additional scrutiny
yet many others glaringly intimidate
and dehumanize him. Their doubts for
his traveling to routine destinations
on vacations, on journeys to living his life
cast aspersions on his refusal to assimilate.
His bright turban, turns their cautionary
gaze, impelling them to demand
adherence. They ask him to take off
his turban at the fancy airports
celebrating diversity with humongous,
exotic frames of ethnic faces and
concrete smiles plastered and painted
on walls. "Only a routine check-up, Sir!"
smirkingly mutters one of them. He smiles
calmly yet refuses the exhibition demanded.
"Not here, never!" He asks for other ways to
alleviate their doubts. "Why do they come here
caring so much about the head nonsense?"
they mutter. He follows them with a calm fury
to another panopticon of surveillance.
"They do not understand," he thinks,

patting down his own turban with
affection and respect, holding out
his hands to their suspicious scrutiny
and mechanized screening.
Someday they will...

He collects his belongings,
wondering about such unbelonging.
They do not understand
those traditions and histories,
those memories and chronicles
of sacrifices and affirmation,
brave resistance and resilience,
against conversion and assimilation.
Someday, he hopes, they will learn
to tolerate turbans, the crowns of
commitment to defend and stand tall.

Till then he must educate the errors,
tell them his reasons. Someday they will
accept his desire to follow, to cherish
this tradition of belonging and promise.
Someday they will...

An Aftermath

A tsunami comes in without warning
a barrage of coldness deluges with shocks
drowning senses with grief and loss unimagined –
such painful unpredictability of inhuman cruelty.
Like white waves gnashing the rocks of faith
then receding finally and we see the remnants
the broken shells, and dark weeds of hate and racism
laying naked on the bare, bloodied sand
and staring coldly at us while we hold vigils
and prayers for those innocent souls gone.

The politicians, analysts and explainers formulate
and fix responses and whataboutery, the hows
and the ifs, the whats and the whys of these violent waves.
Some normalize the damage, others buoyantly play
the blame game from their lofty lighthouses secure.
The mourners wail and wallow, questioning tearfully
such painful unpredictability of inhuman cruelty.
The looming darkness leads to a new dawn as
crimson rays bring kind souls together picking up pieces
of wreckage and loss, still grateful for this beautiful world.

aphasia

furies unleashed
taboos emboldened
mobs frenzied
agendas disguised
no rhyme or reason
neighbors in treason
fanatic rivalries
dragging victims
ripping hairs
tearing clothes
snatching dupattas
shameful groping
lustful attacking
disgusting honor
stabbing fetuses
unbirthing life
strangling shock
killing chores
clipping beards
garlanding tires
splashing kerosene
smoking cigarettes
forcing cigarettes
afraid lips
horrified eyes
evil smiles
deadly ambers
fiery dragons
rising fire
exhibiting deaths
moving on
teaching lessons

50

looting riches
dancing mayhem
another victim
check marked list
killing more
uncovering hide-outs
revealing informants
discriminating demons
cleaning crews
resuming normalcy
shoveling bodies
dying half-deaths
eternal oblivion
no name victims
unnamed predators
no memorials
buried secrets
reluctant forgetting
ghosted spectacle
erased memories
etched nightmares
punctuated emotions...
failed hope
failed justice
failed ideals
... failed words
failed...
fai...
...

Candlelight Vigils

These candles burning in silence
flickering light and emotions
dripping wax in molten grief
amidst calm sobriety
call us to feel
unspoken feelings of calm gloom
unfelt warmth of unknown hands
unheard silence of meditating souls
unseen glimpses of glimmering trust
unbent resolve of firm faiths
unshed tears of mourning
to cherish
to embrace
to hug
to hold
to absorb
to receive
life's gifts and blessings
life's struggles and conflicts
life's ups and downs
through courage not fear
through hope not despair
no speeches
no tendentious theories
no insidious intent
no rhetoric of reason
no wallowing wounds
only rosaries of remembrance
and beads of blessings
breathing
inhaling
the spirit of love
the spirit of optimism
with peace for all.

History

A dark smudge on that glassy facade
bothers the eye of cautionary present.
To clean all smears and splotches,
they collaborate, codify, hide narratives.
Yet traces of hushed memories,
whisper repressed stories and
invisible apparitions peck from
a slanted gaze. Watering the stubborn
smudge with excess lies, they try
to erase it yet miniscule bacteria
of protest grows and spreads like spilt
milk. Meandering its way, seeking
possibilities and audience,
it finally looms in a revolution
demanding thought, penitence and
belated acknowledgements.
The smudge remains, an apparition
of imagination, untraced yet not vanished
in hoary existence. Haunting with an
absent presence, erased etchings,
ignored knowledge, it continues to
portend the foggy future built
on blotches of omissions.

Dislocations

The Name Game

Don't believe the dead white poet
who asked what's in a name!
For my name is my world rolled
with loves, with dreams, with hopes
that perhaps my parents felt when
they looked at my tiny babyness
whining, fussing, being after being
born – an infant oblivious to this
thing called a name.

Perhaps they thought that I will grow
well and conquer this world with
deeds of kindness. Perhaps they wished
success kissing my feet. Or perhaps
they wished a reminder for me to feel
their blood and of those before them
coursing through my veins. Surely,
they didn't think that in this big jungle
world, there would be people who
would want me to change my name
because it evokes fear of strangeness,
or requires them to exceed a syllable
or two, or perhaps acknowledge another
world and history they thought never was,
or perhaps it reminds them of their
misguided power that once was and
is now almost gone.

So in remembrance, I will
retain my name unchanged– syllables and all
and ask you to learn to utter new sounds
that carry the weight of my ancestral name.

Claiming My Doctorate

Yes, I will claim my doctorate,
those years of intellectual labor.
Yes, I will claim my title and feats,
working arduously and then some.
No white clouds will ever tell me
I cannot shine in my hard-earned glory.
No rocks will poke my feet to stop me
from treading and leaving my footprints.
It is my choice to relent or shine...
No metaphors of privilege will
paternalize me nor corner me
to stow away my brilliance.
Yes, I will claim my doctorate.

Flying into Whiteness

Formulated during a fierce debate
among humans denying and challenging
the actions and business of their lives,
I landed on a sea of deep whiteness
my blackness apparent to all who saw me.
Some laughed, some ridiculed my ambitions,
some marveled the courage of my solitary
speck of blackness that had intruded a white space.
I lingered for some time as I always do
hoping there is no dismissive squashing
that would displace me shockingly
or an irritant attack on my daring puny being.
But no dismissive hand moved me away,
so bored with the white sublime,
I flew away to other worlds.

Unequal

Not all deaths are equal, not all mourning too.
Not all compassions are equal, not all sympathies too.
Not all activisms are equal, not all rebellions too.
Not all protests are equal, not all anger too.
Not all regrets are equal, not all reparations too.
Not all violations are equal, not all reprimands too.
Not all aspirations are equal, not all failures too.

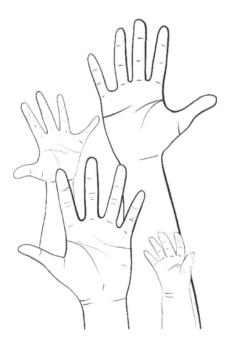

Never Enough

> "So, here you are too foreign for home
> too foreign for here. Never enough for both."
> – Ijeoma Umebinyuo

Walking down the memory lane, I see
a shadow, an apparition from another past:
a forgotten ghazal from youthful days.
Memories, like pieces of an incomplete
puzzle, struggle to belong
hesitatingly whisper to me.
"Will you ever sing us? Remember us?"
Those squiggly uncomposed lines,
nudge me to recall that home I lost.
Thoughts chug out as painful birth
of an impending doubt,
those images from homes bygone
haunt me as an unwound clock.
I begin to remember but my thoughts evaporate
before utterance of feelings for
my foreignness of being never enough.

A tug of war

So, it seems like a tug of war –
I try to balance my multiple pulls
and pushes from a life known there
to a life lived here.
Many homes, many languages,
many ideas, many apparels,
many flavors, many experiences
many privileges, and many prejudices
dislocate and relocate me. I sometimes
swirl like a spinning top until
dizzy spells bring me to my
ultimate reality as the top slows
down, staggering like a blind woman
lost in a maze, resigning her failed ambition
to venture forth. Stuck between nostalgia
and glory of the past, I wait for the promise
of a future when you will finally tell me:
yes, you belong with us,
yes, this is indeed your home.

Living with Hyphens in a Writer's Block

A thought pokes me...
    a prisoner of night and day
        I feel and imagine
            those tedious labyrinths
                the contours of unshaped words
                    of my minds, my memories, my homes.

A memory pokes me...
    a shadow of times bygone
        I yearn with nostalgia
            those moments of innocence
                the lessons of experiences
                    of my lives, my selves, my personas.

A dream pokes me...
    a hazy fog of visions
        I see and unsee
            those strange wanderings
                the spaces filled and hollowed
                    of my hopes, my desires, my prospects.

I stare at the blank screen with no words...
    to write about living with hyphens
        a writer's block – they call it
            those weird ramblings
                the fuzzy silhouettes from times bygone
                    of my shocks, my traumas, my losses.

How do I let words fly in
when they refuse to initiate the journey
to the point of destination?
Like a toddler refusing a stranger's lap,
pouting its lips outward before tears well up
its beautiful eyes, words tug me, hug me
and finally drug me towards a resounding silence.

I Too Will Sing America: A Dream with Langston Hughes[4]

Yesterday Langston came to me
in a dream. Beaten in hate, I laid
in Harlem. With caution, he pulled
my bruised, frail body up. Following his
footsteps, I measured hope and courage
with each stride as a rhapsody ensued.

"I know you- I hear you- I see you.
Like me, pining those dreams for freedom
you rise above the scorching gaze
of otherness. My melodies of pain
from yesteryears are your poetry of justice
today. Sing on, my friend, rise!
Let the optimistic notes
soothing my hungry soul
inspire your brave spirits too.
Your symphony of respect
and rhythms of compassion
will resound and heal those
arrhythmic hearts full of hate.
Sing on, my friend from different
shores, the zenith portends a
colorful dawn with hues of humanity
acknowledging your difference,
appreciating our sameness.
Embracing ignorant fools,
that know not you yet,

---

[4] In September 2013, a Sikh American professor named Prabhjot Singh became victim of a hate crime in Harlem, NY when he was attacked by a crowd of young Islamophobic men.

you too will sing America.
Till then live well, serve well
and sing well."

I wake up from the punches
of reality. Brushing off
the dust of xenophobia, warding off
those splinters of racism, I remember
my roots of gratitude, and embrace all
hues with a promise to walk on
with courage to defeat ignorance.

Go Home!

They tell me "go home!"
But I live here, doing as Romans in Rome.
Looking for better worlds and dreams.
My ancestors, like theirs, left regimes.
Traveling vast continents and deep seas,
In search of that cool, homely breeze.
They squirm at my skin brown
As if it must bring a dubious frown.
They tell me "go home" for my skin isn't right
I am only dark matter, a devil who isn't white
I breathe and exhale as they often do,
Yet they try to choke me till I am all blue.
I am un-homed from my circumstances
with their stares and devious glances.
I smell their rancid revulsions,
On parks, malls and airports' compulsions.
You think like them that home is where the heart is,
No, no, I simply whisper in echoes their angry hiss.

Unhomeliness: A Walk at the Beach

A solitary, luminous flake
peering out of the sandy shroud
seeks me. Demanding a nod at its
passive being, unnoticed by
countless beach swimmers, its
sun-kissed glare dazzles me,
invites me closer.

I drag my callous feet
and feel its brittleness.
An invisible bond
between fractal fragments,
My toes shield its sheer
flimsiness, an ephemeral
moment whispers before
the waves wash away
this fragile rhapsody.

The waves swash over
my age-dried feet protecting
the flake, from cold water's duel
with the hot sand. Distracted from
the luminous, fragile fragment
I find a displaced, duplicitous seaweed,
mapping desperately, tangling my foot
with claws of anguish.

It pleads me to hold on
as I wait for the final drowning.
A thought jitters.
I wrench the terrible weed off
my trembling feet, refusing to budge

to its dark, shapeless thoughts or
wait for the waves to violently reclaim us.

Another emptiness washes my naïve feet
 with a new urgency, calling me to
leave the ground beneath
and cuddle the liquid warmth
enfolding the chilly waves
that draw lunatic thoughts.

A dead bird warns me of the impending
danger in this deadly embrace.
Dead fish on the shore call my name
no comfort for their open blank eyes.
My unwavering feet stand firmly
as I see another luminous flake
washed in the annals of eternity.

I do not embrace this motion of death
and walk onto the still glances of life instead.
Choosing to live on with my fragilities
I leave these ephemeral temporalities
bathing in dark luminosities and join
those crowds of nature-lovers.

Mirage

They told me lies about my greatness
that I was a worthy asset,
someone of value.
I followed them appeased
through dark uncertain alleys.
They pursued me, invited me.
I believed them and kept on believing
trying to belong. Giving everything
and more despite those hesitations,
I followed them unflinchingly.
They brought me to a treacherous hill
demanding a Sisyphean climb.
I hobbled carrying my burden of proof.
Playing safe, uncertain games,
they showed me clouds
and asked me to decipher them.
When the clouds disappeared,
they liked another fresh vapor,
welcomed another haze.
They simply moved on with their
fake smiles, leaving me in lurch
without even a goodbye. I come down
and again meet another group.
They also tell me they like me and ask
me to follow them, again up the hill
looking for a cloud to decipher.
I follow them in awkward meetings
of mistrust, knowing they will tell me in
retrospect what I know already:
I do not belong with them.

Musings in a Museum

I am not so sure if
History speaks the truth.
He smiles that devious smile
And you get seduced by that
fake charm. You want to write
about me with that seductive embrace
that fixes my body in manacles.
A narrative written by you
framed within your realities,
can't tell my story.

Do I dare to even speak up?
Or simply surrender my voice forever?
Your actions cannot be my deeds
Your hypothesis cannot be my realities.
How do you then tell others about me,
my community, my culture and my history?
How do you then interpret my silences,
echo my whispers, hush my utterances?
How do you draw my contours,
form my hazy silhouette
with no details or aspects?
I remain only a shadow
to be seen in your light

And to vanish with your flight.
An artful display in a museum,
my history – a mere object
for quick perusing, a mere foreplay
for your desires for otherness.
I stand alone amidst your audience–
their oohs and ahhs blocked by the
thick plexiglass do not look at
my dried tears for my kind.

Girlhood

Stones in my pockets

Have you walked with young feet
on the vast road by the cotton fields
holding your little sister's nimble
finger showing her the crimson sun
setting, its yellow splendor been eaten
by the orange and red colors like a dragon
swallowing a cough drop? Well, I have.

Showing my curious sister those
pretty cotton flower buds growing by
the side of the ground beneath our feet,
I would tell her how she is like a white
square of softness and one day
her petals will change from creamy white
to yellow, then blushing pink to finally
dark bloody red boll. I do not tell her
that one day we wither and fall
leaving green pods for the harvester to
prod our fibers of being.

She is too young, yet I must teach
her the business of life. At least she
knows why I walk carrying stones
in my pocket to save her and me from
those leery lusty eyes in the field
watching us walk the big road to
watch the crimson sun drown
in its dark majesty.

A Woman's Stones

No, she is not a goddess of stone
even though some worship her.
Simply a clunk of human flesh –
that can't dream because her eyes
are filled with so many stones.
When she is born, regrets ensue
curses following her in poverty,
shame poking her in wealth,
and fear jamming her in-between.
Fear – that demon– chisels her
body with locks, chains and cages.

She carries the rock of violence on
her back -a Sisyphean task sometimes
when they stone her to death with
stones of words. Whack! Wham! Bang!
Casting aspersions, they burn her alive
if she ever did accuse, a cindering Cinderella.
Throwing acid on her if she ever
refused, cracking caustic rain
on her soft stoned skin that crumbles
within– suffocating her silence before she
gives up. Dying, a piece of stone-cold dead
meat that cannot accuse, cannot refuse.

If she lives on, new stones are hurled—
curses, shames, and fears—
blames, guilts and tears –
Her body must have provoked
her clothes must have revealed
her smile must have evoked
her breathing must have invoked

the rapacious intent of men with
uncontrollable urges to powerate
their manliness. Her body is puffed with
those stoned gazes formulating her
femininity into some cause or reason
to blame her stony being.

A Good Girl

Growing up, a "good" Indian girl,
inherits many strictures of
a toddling, barricaded child.
Waiting patiently
while the boys and men ate,
with a perseverant maturity of
a fish in the living room aquarium.
Starving with alimentary constraints,
and lesser wants of
a bird in a cage.
Repressing ambition and opportunities
wearing a veil of domesticity and
jinxed aspirations of a wall lizard.
Asphyxiating aspirations in bubbled existence,
with passive reticence of
an enclosed, running hamster.
Yet exiling frustrations
of a cornered rat, lost in a maze,
when she escapes
restrictive normalcy and
speaks against stone-blind customs,
she is branded a wrecked mind,
a rabid dog better discarded.

An Unwritten Letter[5]

Mother, do you ever think about us?
your aborted, unlived daughters
who dared to grow within you
but never came to be.

Mother, do you ever cry for us?
Our undreamed aspirations simply quashed by
your hateful silence, your murderous complicity
to banish us from your womb for that imperative birth of a
boy.

Mother, did you not hear our hearts beat?
with pulsating rhythm, did you not see our
silhouette and shadows floating on that monitor screen
when the doctor scoped us to find our sex?

Mother, do you ever imagine us?
How we could have lived and grown
How we could have loved if not thrown
away into infested purgatory of non-being.

Do you even feel our pain of separation?
Will you ever read this unwritten letter
from all of us—me and my other unborn sisters
who met the same fate
sucked out like an unwanted weed
evicted forcibly with our pathetic placentas
smothering our unformed beauty
because we did not come with that

---

[5] This poem is a response to the rampant female feticide in some
cultures which is induced by privileging birth of sons to daughters.

coveted mark of maleness
with promises of generations beyond?

Mother, do you remember us? Mother, do you remember
those pounds of your flesh?

Sister Love

These gracious words of yours, dear sisters!
Bring memories of cackles, dear sisters!
Our resounding, peeing laughter, dear sisters!
Whispering after snubs and rebukes, dear sisters!
happiness drenching us all, dear sisters!
I am waiting again for those warm meetings, dear sisters!
For deep ruminations and wisely counsel, dear sisters!
Your pampering me with your love, dear sisters!
Advising me to care for myself, dear sisters!
Wiping my worries with hugs of dearness, dear sisters!
Assuring me of support and life's graces, dear sisters!
I am waiting again for those warm meetings, dear sisters!

Resistance

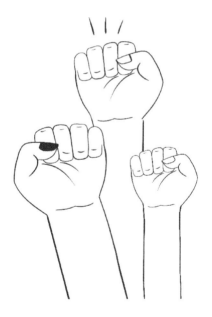

On Wings of Their Words

The neoliberal puppet masters
try to infiltrate with the emperor's rigamarole
in razzle dazzle. Garish puppets dance
on hollow tunes of shiny hogwash
about glittering façade of change,
glorifying sagas of progress with
ultramodern backdrop boasting how
the nation must welcome a new dawn.

Myriad puppets slander in a borrowed
monotone how these farmers must
be anti-national, eating pizza,
speaking good English and resisting
corporate breadcrumbs of prosperity.
Brave farmers have united recognizing the
devious puppetry of golden strings that
divide and control. Unimpressed by
sassy narratives of false histories and
imaginary futures, they have perched
on trolleys, tractors with tarpaulins to march
and fly on wings of their words and
claim the roads, poised to inherit open
skies to sing in unison their own narratives,
chant prayers of hope and poetry of valor
to dream a world of kindness free
from golden strings and corporate chains
of the devious puppet masters.

To hope perchance to dream

These tired eyes have seen all
beyond those shadows in the cave
and hollowed echoes that you
believe to be real. Yet they
dream for new imaginings for a world
that can scan our hopes and visions
not in a mechanical panopticon
through far-off images from the telescope
to wonder, nor those still, remote and
forgettable images from the bioscope.
Instead, these tired eyes hope perchance to
dream a world where you can come down
from your golden cages and join us at
these revolutionary grounds. A world where
you don't see us as parasites but fellowmates
with pain in these eyes, and so join us to
soothe our fears and wipe our tears.

A Clarion Call

Behold, these brave farmers
marching on with dreams,
dissenting in chilly Delhi!

Carrying courageous histories on
burdened backs, erasing ignorance
with humility, seizing those twinkling
fireflies, they hope for an unfettered
morrow. To dispel the foggy futures of
their children, their protests
imagine a world glistening with
justice. Confidently they speak up,
resounding a clarion call.

Newsmakers seem distracted by their age
and wrinkles. Some want to hijack their
voice, some ridicule their courage with sharp
darts of insults and arrows of fearful rhetoric.
They do not know their warrior histories...

Many have joined in unison to amplify
their calls for justice. Others have thrown
spears of doubt from high ivory
windows to stab in the back.
Yet bravely they speak up to live on.

Will revolutionary wheels burrow into
fallow minds to germinate
new fruits of labor? Or will they simply
be stuck in secret rabbit holes?
Will voices resound with ripples
of radical love? Or simply fizzle

by cacophonies of elitism
diluting their logic of justice?
Are there hopes in their dreams—
or simply fuzzy castles in air?

Today We Rise On

They think they can hold us afraid and down,
chained in a cave of dark shadows brown.
Instead we must come out to see the light
waiting to embrace us in love and might.
They think we can forget our callous suppression
the hangman tightening the noose after false confessions.
Instead we remember those disappeared in haste
even the last breath exhaled in unknown waste.
They think they can lead us as passive, meek herds
Instead we resist cowering, and lionize as free birds.
They think they can color us copper brazen
with mischievous, blind strokes of devious abrasions.
Instead we gleam through in golden hues and rays
an artist's pure imagination to peruse and marveled gaze.
They think they can speak for us in hollow cacophony,
Instead we resound our own narratives of symphony.
They think they can concoct and spread a liar's tale
Instead we weave truth with threads of courage to prevail.
They think they can tear the pages of our warrior souls
instead we heal soothing our hearts heavy with grievous tolls.
They think they can condemn us, beat us, hush us,
hurt us with smears, and even cruelly crush us.
Instead we gather all differences together
to speak, to be heard, and seen in fair measure.
Abandoning fear and darkness we simply march on
the righteous path, yes, today we rise on,
to claim our rightful share and to live and adorn
a haven of strength for all born and yet to born.

Sikhi

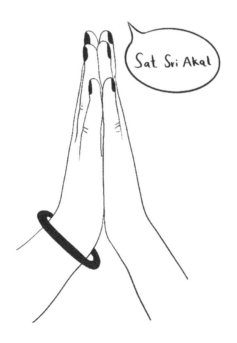

That Dark Dawn

As morning opens its beak
and drinks the sunshine nectar,
crimson rays erase shadows
of last night's darkness.
Hushed memories flutter their wings
and recall that sacrilege today.
Divine music graces, as it did then,
a sacred ambiance pours devotion
into those thirsty, faithful ears.

The hustling love, the bustling charm
effuses admiration, as devotees
enjoy the cool breeze. Washing away
doubts, multitudinous feet throng
toward that serene, sacred hub of
incredible grace. The waters shimmer,
the fish gaze. Devotees splash feet,
hands, eyes, all mesmerized by that
grand reflection. A purity sops up the
darkness within. So many feet
sipping self-surrender, so many hands
folded in humility, as they enter this haven.

Hundreds feeling blessed – in
this gracious company of
the initiated and the seekers.
The mesmerizing charisma,
the rhapsodic aura allures,
and invites them all over.
Thousands of feet tread softly
recalling those splinters of history
those unforgotten pasts. Those

scabrous blemishes call them today
to remember those horrific wounds of
unfathomable indignity.

II

The pitter-patter of a child's running feet
around the parkarma, echoes a rhythmic beat.
The hurried feet of his worrisome mother scramble.
She embraces him as his sun-blushed cheeks
remind her of her long-gone brother, who
died somewhere here amidst the barrage of bullets.
The slow-paced, calloused feet of an old man
remind him of those youthful days of happiness
now a mere melancholic mirage. His solitude
accentuates his memories of a young son lost
in oblivion, unknown, unlived, and branded by
unseen danger. He wonders about those
grandchildren denied to him, their chance to
walk today with him in enchanted bliss.
His tears-filled eyes still find peace, wisdom
and celestial guidance in autumnal days of his life.
The arthritic feet of an old woman supported by wheels,
pace slowly. She remembers those days when she raced
as a child the same parkarma with her sisters.
She remembers her childhood before bullets pierced
their convictions, before her baby sisters drowned in that
bloodied pool. Her feet, like history, struggle a
burdened gait stooping to pick up those unseen
shards of memories.

The henna-painted feet of a shy bride in red
walk beside her handsome groom
seeking blessings with humility and faith

crossing life's threshold of marital bliss.
She hopes new desires as her feet follow
her partner on this path of exquisite
commitment. Today, she remembers
her grandfather she never saw and imagines him
walking the parkarma before those bullets
riddled him off. Pressing her feet firmly
on the shiny granite she imagines touching
his invisible footprint somewhere on this periphery.

III

Today slumberous history awakens and roars
as our multitude of feet tread gently while
teased by cool splashes on hot marble designs.
It becks and calls for a rejuvenation,
an affirmation. Washing away doubt,
with serene purity, our water-kissed feet
stride in steadfast faith. Despite those marks
of unforgotten intrusions, despite those testimonies
of trauma, we all bow down to the supreme love,
praying with humble hands – in ardaas,
a petition with those nimble fingers
caressing silent reminiscences
and prayers for martyrs.
We ask for hope and strength,
for remembrance and resilience,
for commitments and promises
to memorialize that dark dawn which
hatched upon those pilgrims a crimson
cacophony of military bombardments
painful decades ago.

Breaths of Life

Each breath we inhale and exhale—
A testimony to our gifts—
To feel the cool breeze
To see beauty in all its majesty
To hear the music of living
To taste the bounties of kindness
To whiff the aromas of compassion.
Yet we casually ignore and instead heed
To feel a vain superiority
To see shallow differences
To hear echoes of egomania
To taste the entitled privilege
To whiff fallacious stench of racism.
O what a waste, O what a waste!

Shukrana
(To be thankful)

Shukrana, for these breaths of life
    to behold beauty inside and outside.
Shukrana, for great minds provoking us
    to learn our power inside and outside.
Shukrana, for countless reminders
    to reflect and grow inside and outside.
Shukrana, for lessons and experiences
    to feel spirituality inside and outside.
Shukrana, for worthy relationships
    to sense radical love inside and outside.
Shukrana, for all models in our lives
    to inspire kindness inside and outside.
Shukrana, for gratitude today and always
    to live simply inside and outside.

Guru Nanak

When darkness enveloped the minds
through rigid chains of ritualism,
when blind worship thrived
through uncritical observances,
when knowledge remained privileged
in books, not hearts and minds,
a great child philosopher
emboldened by learner's curiosities,
asked his teachers for true knowledge.

Questioning the existing
paradigms of religion,
he brought new meanings
and truths. Spreading the light of wisdom
and equality, the learner became
the humble teacher,
guiding for a community of spiritual focus,
honest life and radical sharing.

The mist and darkness surrendered
and gave way as the world brightened
to a clear common goal to recognize
cosmic worship and to care for all.
Traveling and reaching out,
he taught us to learn critically with compassion
as enlightened souls.

Tassels of Kindness – Bandi Chorr

Today I think of so many prisoners
languishing in dark dungeons of despair
and caves of ignorance
imagining their future dissolve
with unknown consequences
while we light candles thinking
there is no darkness now.

Today I think of that compassionate Guru
whose double swords of sovereign and
spiritual powers helped him
 imagine a future of collective
liberation from the mighty oppressors,
who dreamed to protect his community
from injustice through warrior ethos,
venturing a steel fortress, hoisting the exalted flag
summoning war drums to evoke martial spirits
to resist injustices, to imbue spiritual prowess,
who braved the betrayal of whispering
connivers, fearlessly endured the shackles of prison
refusing to accept a selfish freedom
and offered tassels of kindness to seek
liberation and justice for 52 other prisoners.

Today let us not simply light up candles
that melt into nothingness,
but instead find the flicker
to remind us the fire burning within
to find the dazzling warrior within
to brighten the lives of others
to offer tassels of kindness
so no one is left behind languishing
in dark dungeons of despair
and caves of ignorance.

The Coronation

The image of the Sikh in the mirror,
so appealing, so handsome,
a young prince receiving coronation,
getting ready to face the world.
His freshly-bathed beard,
with curls like wavy clouds
caressed with admiration and care.
His long hair embracing him,
a royal cape of responsibility.

Bowing in admirable and loving service
he gathers these cascades of
black wisps from back to front,
combing out the tangles
through caution, care and affection.
Like life, the Sikh man loves his hair,
with obedience and pride,
following this daily ritual
of remembrance and affirmation.

The soft, shining hair, go with the flow
of his tender, guiding hands.
The strands surrender their movements
kneaded together in unison.
His long beard twirled in grasps
of firmness and glued conviction.
His hair– like faithful subjects
follow the king's wishes,
no rebellion, no insurgence,
a simple complacency
of honor and respect.

The curls and twists and turns
give up to his hand's beckoning.
The tugs strengthen his commitment,
rolling into a confident
knot of circular solidarity,
reminding him of his promise
to cherish God's gift.
The tied band on the forehead
prepares him for this coronation.

Five meters of muslin meanwhile,
caressed and stretched
between him and his wife
affirming their unbreakable
bond, an unwavering commitment.
Twirling the folds inside,
unwrinkling the wraps
with patted caresses,
he glances at his wife
as she twirls the folds on the other side.
She smiles back like a blushing bride
concealing emotions in wrapped layers.

The quick pulls and tugs and folds
bring them closer as they meet
with layers and folds of the crowning,
waiting eagerly to be placed
on the proud head.

The mirror shows him ready for the moment,
he smiles at his beautiful empress.
He reminds her of their wedding
day when she saw her glorious groom
eyeing secretly his new bride.

The first fold embracing his neck,
a corner clenched tightly,
like a child learning to hold with his teeth,
moving up from the back to the forehead
and then sloping down back.
His crown emerges amidst
this affectionate perusing,
these multiple folds
of dedication and tradition
inheritance and reverence,
commitment and allegiance,
a disciple's acknowledgment
of his Guru's edification.

Remembering his Guru's determined call,
he imagines that spring morning
when followers accepted the regal form
to bear and acknowledge the ambrosial
nectar of commitment and promises.
No fear in their hearts,
only a passion for obedience,
valiant soldiers, bold in thought
and actions, they learned to embrace
equality, drinking sips of pious
sweetness immersed with the Guru's love.

The Sikh man's smile reveals
the same pride of ancestral promises
as he sifts through his mirror-image
getting ready to face the world
that knows not yet of his cherished inheritance.
The proud wife wonders if
the world will ever know about

the hidden tunnels and histories
of arduous persecutions.
Will they ever unearth these
grandiose, invisible rubies of faith and
jewels of optimism adorning his crown?
Bidding wishes and love
to her handsome prince,
she hopes they will understand
perhaps someday... if not today
surely someday.

Vaisakhi 1699

Imagine a community of believers
gathered at Anandpur Sahib on Vaisakhi
to listen faithfully to their Guru's wisdom.
The plume-adorned Guru dazed them
like a bolt of lightning on a sunny day
a poet philosopher inspiring his listeners
with a clarion call, simply demanding a willful
surrender of self — a readiness to give up self-worship.

Imagine those five beloveds
from different creeds and castes:
a shopkeeper, a farmer, a tailor,
a water-carrier, a barber who
rose up to the call for solemn sacrifice.
Fearless with faith to meet the Guru's sword,
they stepped up to follow him unquestioningly
ready to surrender their lives for the Guru.

Imagine as the Guru brought
his beloved disciples back – the glorious Khalsa
adorned in his image nurturing compassion,
righteousness, courage, strength and humble grace
to follow the path of oneness and fellowship
to resist tyranny, to defend social justice
to serve humanity with selfless love
and to promote compassion for all.

Imagine such wonder of selfless love
embracing thousands of seeking souls.
A sweet immersion into a promise
of compassionate connections initiated
the five beloveds as they sipped the sweet Amrit.

The Guru then bowed for his own initiation –
Guru became disciple – his palms joined blissfully
to drink the sweetened sword-dipped nectar.

Imagine such undying legacy of humanity as
the Guru gifted his disciples with 5 Ks, names and
purpose, asking Sikhs to relinquish rituals, forego taboos,
cast-off castes, renounce superstitions and unshackle their
minds from divisions. Instead, assume a unique identity –
to be courageous Singhs and Kaurs practicing equality,
and creating a world of freedom and revolutionary love
where no one is superior nor deemed inferior.

The Pandemic

When we come out of this

When we come out of this...
Will we be wiser or simply resume our privileges?
Will we be kinder or simply defend our selfism?
Will we be thoughtful or simply forget our helplessness?
Will we be grateful or simply brag our survival?
Will we be compassionate or simply assign fate to the unfortunate?
Will we be ethical in choices or simply drench with entitlement?
Will we accept our common vulnerabilities or simply blame with hate-mongering?
Will we learn to persist with humility to help others or simply demand callous liberation to serve our enabled egos?
Will we come out of this or simply languish in philosophy or poetry?

To be or not to be masked: Hamlet's Covid soliloquy
(with apologies to the Bard)

To be or not to be masked, that is the question:
Whether it is nobler in the mind to suffer others
Your slings and arrows of outrageous droplets,
Or to take arms against a logic of kindness
And by opposing end it. To die—alone,
No more; and by a careless horror we begin
The heartache and the thousand natural shocks
That infected flesh is heir to: it's a consummation
Never to be wished. To die away from loved ones.
To suffer, perchance to breathe—ay, there's the rub:
For in that breath of death what dreams may come
To end, when others have shuffled off this mortal coil.
Must give us pause to reflect —there's the respect
That makes calamity of so many suffering unknowingly.
For who would bear the whips and scorns of time,
The asymptomatic oppressor's wrong, the proud man's
contumely,The pangs of arrogant self-love, the right to
breathe unmasked. The insolence of office, and the spurns
That privileged merit the unmasked takes,
When he himself might his quietus make
With a bare, poisonous exhale?
Who would the burden bear,
To grunt and sweat amidst this virulent air,
But that the dread of untimely, lonely death,
The undiscovered life, from whose lap
We all wish to swing, puzzles the will,
And makes us rather courteous to prevent
those ailments we have than fly to others that
we know not of. Thus, conscience does make
kindred of us all, and the native hue of resolution

Is sicklied over with the somber cast of thought,
And fear of great calamity and moment
With this regard their currents turn awry
And accept the kindness – to nobly wear the
masks after all. —So cover up now!
Let the deadly Corona be banished and in thy prayers,
Be all its sins remembered.

When Contagion Comes

When contagion comes, it brings
swarms of mistrust and alarms of fear,
wells of ignorance and quells of emotions,
winds of despair and rims of misery,
pleas of caution and sprees of vigils,
orders of distance and borders of travel,
hoarding of wares and eroding of affairs,
doubting of dreams and waiting for vaccines,
bouts of paranoia and clouts of dismissal...
and yet when contagion comes, it also brings
aromas of kindness and fragrance of service
sweetness of philanthropy and salty relief,
comforts of patience and caresses of care,
whispers of gentleness, and sighs of love
glimmers of hope, and shimmers of fellowships,
we wait, and we wait for the ebbs and the flows
we wait, and we wait for the contagion finally leaving
us kinder if not wiser. Yes, we wait...and write
and hope to live on while we wait.

Another Contagion

So your masks have come off and shown your
devious minds, your privileged world
of paranoia and contagious infections—
negating human connections, you live in bubbles
of selfness. Shirking away in fear, you dread
their vicinities in ignorance drowned in feverish
ghastly thoughts, you imagine in hate how their
impure breathing will pollute you, endanger you.
You don't want them in your communities and
congregations, loving yourselves too much.
You can't smell the stink of putrid racism simmering
in cauldrons of your rancid logic. It is exhausting
with excruciating aches and pains that you can't feel
because your lethargic minds simply languish in
the beliefs of your rightness. You sanitize yourself
from pollutants unaware of your disgusting phobia
that violates others. Perhaps there will someday
come a cure of this infection that has congealed your
privilege, perhaps there will someday come a cure that
will allow you to breathe in kindness to all. Till then
they hope and till then they write hoping you
will look in the mirror and remember those eyes
you failed to look, those faces covered in
masks of generosity you so easily overlooked.
Perhaps someday...

Pandemic Lessons

So, I asked my students in the zoom class:
what have you learned in this pandemic?
Any deep insights? Any flickering revelations?
Any rueful regrets? Any wanton wishes?
A silence ensued... for two seconds...
an ellipsis of calm turmoil.

I waited with bated breath... like bubbles
disappearing in a fizzling drink wondering
what these young minds would tell me
from beyond their virtual boxes with
backgrounds of untraveled places.
And then I saw a stream of messages
filling the chat-box with ebullience
of red ants rushing out seeking new directions,
new outlets beyond the rims
of passivity. The messages poured
themselves quenching the unknown
thirst being sequestered in a sprawling desert.
Slowly, they began to share what they
learned forcefully from this pandemic:
who their real friends are – checking their
well-being in a text, in a call, in language of care,
 how they are never alone or have
learned to be alone in new realities, how to pay attention
to minds and bodies, in gratitude and face masks,
how compassion is sacred and crucial for their
community like the air they breathe and
hope to survive and focus on things that matter
not the norms that bind them,
how it takes a village to save lives,
how less introvert they are now than they
thought, how long late-night drives helped them
clear their heads of brain fog and burnout,

to cherish small interactions, the hellos
and the hi's that validate them to smile and believe,
that yes, they are still alive and healthy,
to cherish the time spent with families helping them
pass this one day at a time, how they should have
learned to manage their money without the trappings
between paychecks, should have invested more in stocks,
checked in on their friends before they passed away,
to pray and find solace for themselves and loves they lost,
to appreciate life and holding its flimsy threads,
to paint the beauty of this world before it evaporates,
to watch basketball games in nostalgia for crowded places,
to seek support and save themselves from inner demons,
to surround themselves with good people who made them
laugh, getting through, feeling alive in this pandemic.

The brimful emotional cup of my chat box showed me
invisible tears and silent whispers for unknown fears,
hoary sighs for a lifestyle lost in the labyrinths,
beautiful smiles of resilience too—
so many responses these young minds shared,
about their foggy futures and silver linings.
Soon it is time to log off yet they patiently wait until I thank
them in gratitude about living the business
of life with death looming outside and close by.
They sign off in solidarity and one by one
those boxes disappear until I look at my lonely face
staring at me from the zoom cage imploring me to
end this meeting with no one there. I think in
humility how to write a poem capturing these
emotional nuances and vagaries and quietly
log off – a teacher in appreciation of so many
pandemic lessons learned from my students.

About the Author

Dr. Parvinder Mehta is a Sikh American poet with a Ph.D in English from Wayne State University, USA, on Asian American women's writings.

This book is the author's debut poetry collection. Dr. Parvinder Mehta currently teaches undergraduate writing and literature courses in Detroit, Michigan.

Made in the USA
Middletown, DE
02 November 2023

41803645R00070